The Residue of Heartbreak

BookLeaf
Publishing
India | USA | UK

Jasmin Chmaisse

Presentation by *BookLeaf Publishing*

Web: www.bookleafpub.com

E-mail: info@bookleafpub.com

ISBN: 9789360941321

First edition 2024

VOLUME 1

Chapter 1

I won't justify the words that

caused you to step away.

They were words of anger

I remember to this day.

I know I am not innocent.

I know that when you leave you mean to be
gone forever.

But your absence makes my heart ache.

If only regret could take back the words I said
that day…

Maybe you'd be here with me, as I ask you to
stay.

Stay for a very long time.

Chapter 2

God if I deserve better then

make him the "better" I deserve.

Chapter 3

When I think of perfect,

   I don't think of you.

       \-   Your thoughts of me when you
           left.

Chapter 4

I view sunsets way too often,

feel the coldness of the sea,

but drift away deeper into it,

carefree.

I listen to the melodies the centuries gave me

and lose myself in the words that raised me.

I take photographs of the things I want to remember,

and keep them safe for they are ageing's treasure.

I laugh with the people who stood by me,

and cry when they are in agony,

because the best people in life,

the very best people

always suffer tremendously.

I travel and wander like a lost cause

searching for something it can be.

But then I remember,

you are missing from me.

You see, I can fill my life up

with all those extravagant experiences and views

but nothing is ever able to replace you.

- You are my greatest adventure.

Chapter 5

Too much of his absence

is too much of a pain for me.

-    Let me leave.

Chapter 6

Missing you

is now engraved in me.

Sometimes I can't feel it directly,

but the sadness that resulted from your absence,

has captured my chest and has made itself

a permanent resident.

The things I have from you now

besides the memories,

are so minimal.

This sadness reminds me of you way too often.

But what if this pain means something.

Would it matter to you?

\-   Maybe this pain could be proof
that I am the one for you.

Chapter 7

I know I am young.

I know that I know so little of this world's hurt.

But you my darling,

make me feel everything so very deeply.

And if what I am feeling now is nothing,

    Then so be it.

Chapter 8

Can love change an unsteady heart?

-   Maybe if the answer was "yes," I wouldn't be here writing this.

Chapter 9

I've forgotten how it feels like to be fine.

Chapter 10

Sending me off to hell I see.

But haven't I broken enough hearts,

to show you that it's worthy?

Worthy of a second chance.

Chapter 11

I am not looking for normal.

I am looking for you.

-   I don't even pray for myself
    anymore. You are always my
    wish.

Chapter 12

It shouldn't be about

you returning the hurt.

It should be about you

moving on.

Chapter 13

If I do not express my feelings

then my heart would never forgive me.

- I love you but you make me sad.
- I love you but you are no good for me.

Chapter 14

Maybe if I show up with

blood stains all over my dress,

you'd ask me if I'm fine?

- You are always the best I've ever had but lost.

Chapter 15

So here's the thing,

there's these brown eyes I'm in love with,

beautifully made like a brown and white parade.

Their look honors you,

as if you were the only girl in the world,

born anew.

You used to tell me that I was a big part of you.

How your lungs were filled up with the air that I breathe

and how your veins had memorized the sound of my laugh,

as they pumped that soul of yours.

But here I am,

gasping for air, as the sounds of nothingness beat the drums in my ear.

Because dare I say it, you stopped being near.

And as I sold my soul to whatever you owned, everything turned into a blur.

I just wanted to know how you were, and what you were doing.

If I cannot make you mine, then I will stay in the shadows arguing with god about my evildoing.

Chapter 16

What about all the things you wished for?

There came a time when you wished for me;

when you wished that I'd be the girl you'd wake up with and love.

Don't just leave a wish come true.

Chapter 17

What am I supposed to do with

        all the love you've built in me?

-    I am

        an old feeling

            to him.

Chapter 18

I leave a piece of myself

in everything I write.

So maybe that's why you wouldn't even look me
in the eye.

Chapter 19

When you feel so greatly

and so passionately about someone,

then waiting is unnecessary.

> \- I look for you in daylight as well.

Chapter 20

Is it because of me?

Or is it because of you, that we forgot to fly?

-     The answer I was trying to escape is this: you always flew away without me. You then flew back to me after long periods of time. Each time you'd come back, you'd fill me up with hope again that one day soon, we'll fly away together. But this time, you took off for good. I want to tear off my wings now and learn how to walk.

Chapter 21

I remember the rush I had

before meeting at noon.

Getting away with my words,

patiently waiting for the moment I get to see you.

You arrived and it was like,

you've come to tell me good news.

The door opened for you and your smile lit up.

As it was getting brighter and wider,

you leaned in closer with your hands spread open.

I thought to myself, he knows I never want him to leave right?

Did you really think,

that I would ever forget such a welcome?

You grew your smile in my heart.

And as it's getting older,

It's sticking its pictures up all over my mind and memories.

I remember…

God damn it I remember everything.

I wonder if all these words are being wasted on you.

I wonder if these words,

make any sense to you.

Must I show you what I think of you?

Or shall I only tell the moon?

Because after you were gone,

he was the only thing I had left.

The closest thing to the brightness of your smile.

Do I tell you how the color gray

matched your body so perfectly?

Or do I tell you how you looked like when you were happy;

when you saw me, for the very first time?

Do I tell you how much you've grown in me?

Or do I tell you,

how much you've made me lose, from myself?

Chapter 22

My darling,

Love was in my arms

but you were afraid.

I told you,

I am not the pain in your past

nor the sins you regret.

I wanted to be the person

you wake up to in 47 years.

I am here now,

and I am telling you, I love you.

Chapter 23

I will carry your soul in my heart.

The same heart you helped me build.

Chapter 24

He once told me, "I don't need to dwell too much about what you've done or who you've been with. Nor will I ask you about the things you regret. We've all made mistakes and now the past is behind us, let us focus on what's coming."

-    A lover I never got over

It was finally me with him. Not the me I wasn't proud of. It was just me, and it was just him.

Chapter 25

I've gotten through the process

of losing you so many times…

I know how it feels like.

Yet every time I think of losing you again,

my heart drops and I can't breathe.

My heart starts to grieve.

I've asked you enough times,

to not take me in as your prisoner when all you
ever do is treat me like your unwanted sinner.

Chapter 26

Love does not mean I have to kiss you to feel it.

Love means I can look at you for one minute and feel it.

-    100,000 sayings thrown I almost said to you.

Chapter 27

Not having you in my life

is like an ill child,

not having his mother beside him throughout the
night,

not even having her throughout all the days that
follow as well.

Chapter 28

Now it's time for me

to romanticize myself

kicking you out of my life.

-       You burned my heart.

Chapter 29

And just like a traveler,

      you were off to new things.

-    Why wasn't I your sweet serenity?

Chapter 30

They tell you:

"Do not dare say that you are incomplete without him."

Bullshit.

Bullshit.

I do feel incomplete.

I don't feel the same.

Not that I am less of a person,

But he was a lot to me.

I decide what I feel and why.

When I die,

there will be people to tell my tale.

A look into my past, where once lived a glorified human being

who left a heart so frail,

because he did not know how to love her

his selfish would prevail.

As she sat near her portal, waiting for him to return,

a minute just like the other,

you'd think she'd learn.

Chapter 31

No heart can really take,

what's left after

what you've done to me.

       -   and you aren't coming back to me.

Chapter 32

I broke a heart that loved me so dearly.

I broke his heart because I wasn't over my true love.

But maybe God is showing me,

what my true love feels now towards me,

is what I feel towards the man I broke.

Oh my dear lord,

allow me to be the loyal lover

of the man I tore down,

in another parallel universe.

But give me my true love in this one.

-    The cost I'd pay to have him now.

Chapter 33

And every time I remember

that you left,

It is like new news to me.

- You are the lie in all my dreams.

Chapter 34

I cannot welcome thoughts of you anymore.

I'm tired.

My heart is worn-out and has trouble beating.

My brain cannot stay wired under your foundation.

Chapter 35

But what would I say

if I saw you someday, for the very first time

in so long?

I used to look at you and think "the world turns green underneath his feet."

But now,

if I were to look at you,

all I will see is pain.

All the nights I spent crying alone over you will flash before my eyes.

Then my heart will break again, just a little.

But not over you.

Over the woman who passed through so much agony and had to go through hell.

Chapter 36

I used to think so highly of you.

Believed you'd stay after saying "I love you."

But then she came along.

Turned that "I love you" into "I'm leaving you
I'm sorry."

So where are you now?

Have you gone to some place better?

A place where the movement of time in the trees

does not whisper to you, my name.

But whisper an eternity,

with her.

Chapter 37

But my mind does not get

why I still have you in my heart.

Chapter 38

I am in love with a boy

who no longer exists.

Sad, isn't it?

- I need you, but I forbid myself
to have you.

Chapter 39

Think of it as, you just ate a big meal and you are full, you can't even breathe.

It almost feels like you will never be able to eat again.

But the truth is, 3, 4 or 5 hours later, you'll start to feel hungry, and you will eat again.

Think of this example in association with the residue of heartache. Say you've had a huge and terrible heartbreak. It feels like you will never be able to love again. But the truth is, after some time, someone along the way will treat you in ways you've never even thought of; and you will start to fall. You will love; and your life will go on.

-    Residue of heartbreak

-    This is the hypocrisy of
the human heart and
body

Chapter 40

So what now I asked?

"now I leave you be."

But this is not fair, I love you…

"sometimes we wish for things but we don't always end up getting what we want."

You can't say that to me… I did not wish for anything but you

"I just can't see you like this anymore, I have my own world and you have yours."

Why'd you come back if you were going to leave me this way?

"I wanted to give us a chance."

A chance?

And did you even think about how all this would affect me if it didn't work out? After you shared that you were not able to live without

me?

"..."

- 2019

Chapter 41

They tell me,

"just when you stop wanting something, it comes back to you."

But I don't know how to not want you.

I can't even get your image out of my head.

If people ask me about you and I tell them, "yes, I have moved on,"

would that help?

They tell me,

"fake it till you make it"

But how can I fake anything when even your name still makes me shiver?

It's been years now…

How can I turn you into a stranger? Tell me.

Chapter 42

I've never had a steady home.

But when it felt like I did,

I wanted to tell the whole world about it.

I guess each tornado blew it away,

and each tsunami washed it away.

I kept trying to fix it.

But then I got tired and realized, not all things wish to be fixed.

Some things aren't even meant to be fixed.

But I couldn't help it…

I was a kid in love.

Chapter 43

Little by little,

I've stood up,

and I have faced what I've been scared shitless from;

your leaving.

I don't know whether I've become desensitized,

Or if I have hidden hope in me that tells me to stay calm now and assures me, unconsciously, that one day

you're coming back to me.

I want to unravel all the tricks,

all the secrets,

that my mind has hidden for you.

I want to dust your name off from every corner of my brain.

I want you out.

I want you gone.

Chapter 44

As all of this comes to an end,

I want you guys to know,

it is okay to admit that you're tired.

It is okay to lean on someone's shoulder and cry every now and then.

It is okay to speak up about your hurt.

Our hearts can never fully rest without closure

and the high volumes it wishes to speak with.

Go on and share your story…

I'm listening.

Chapter 45

I grieved for the person

you were when I loved you,

and moved on.

Chapter 46

And as for him, well;

When the time is right,

I will read you all the poetry I have written

But you must hold courage to your chest.

Goodbye, R

VOLUME 2

Friendship edition

Chapter 1

My Dear,

my apologies extend to the hereafter.

I've missed you.

I did not think for one second that I would ever write a book about you.

Darling, this is where I write down all my sorrows,

all my what ifs and I wishes,

and all the parts of me that are in chronic pain.

Sincerely, I will try and let this be my last attempt to keep you alive in the back of my mind.

- Here's to calling you "My dear, My darling" a 100 times in this book.

Chapter 2

If heaven had a sound,

I would try and capture it just to prove to you,

that the sound of yours could make heaven's one shush.

Do you still laugh as loud?

It's been years since I have made you laugh.

A part of me is hoping that you remember the times that I did.

You used to hide your giggle with the palm of your hand,

squint your eyes,

and let out a laugh even funnier than the joke I made.

I don't think you should hide your laugh
anymore. It was so beautiful I'm here years later
writing about it.

I hope every friend you meet makes you laugh.

I hope at the end of every laugh,

you remember this page.

-    If I had 3 wishes, you would be my
     third.

Chapter 3

I've had three heartbreaks in my life, dear readers.

One of them almost drowned me.

She was there for all three.

She would hug me for the first, take me out for the second, and make sure I was okay under water for the third.

My dear, you are no longer in my life.

I pray no man sinks that treasured heart of yours.

But if it were to happen, would you call me?

Is there still a home in me?

My dear, losing you has broken into my bones,

sending me off to a different ocean.

But if you needed me,

I have myself to pick up, then swim two oceans

to find you.

-    I pray misery sweeps me away than feel
     my sorrows on land.

Chapter 4

It is currently 10:40 PM,

October the 8th, 2023.

I'm in Sydney wishing I was 7,594 miles away.

I am in the comfort of my own home,

but I wish to be 7,594 miles away from it.

I write this with complete and utter sadness,

that I think even if I was 7,594 miles away from home, separated by a wall from you,

I would still be by myself.

- I've knocked on that wall once but to no avail.

Chapter 5

My family is calling.

They have asked about you more than I can bear.

Each time I brush them off with "We're fine, I swear."

I wish that lie was true.

My dear, have you heard of the broken man who lies then believes his own lie?

I think I understand him now.

I can see the weight of the world on his tongue,

as he blurs out what he wishes to be true.

Leaving his reality behind,

for no truth is worth losing someone like you.

-     Manifesting a world with _ _ _ _ _

Chapter 6

You never know what the term "best friend"
means

Until you love someone who is

not your husband nor your daughter.

Not your priest nor your sheikh.

Not the country you would die for,

nor the music that was made for you.

But indeed, it is a person,

that clouds your judgment of life, and turns it
into a field of color.

As weird as that sounds,

my darling, I never noticed the color of dawn,

nor the color of spring flowers until they had
gone.

At times colors were just in the background

Like the colors of rooftops, leaving the gray in
the sky to take effect as the rain drops.

My darling, I didn't even know the touch of
different things

Like the softness of grass, or the window's glass.

But then I felt everything's mass

when I met you.

Chapter 7

My darling, if I drove past your house

in the first car I've ever bought myself,

would you join me?

Or would I just be another stranger in the street,

passing on the concrete?

If that were to ever happen,

then can you lead the way to wherever you
want?

Because the melancholy that comes after the
drive has already sunk into my chest.

So let us make a deal.

I will keep driving,

and you can keep talking.

And when I sink,

you can take the steering wheel.

Chapter 8

I have reached a point in my life

where there are more questions than there are
answers.

More busy days than there are calm ones.

More people to meet than my ability to host
them into my heart like I did with you.

Do not worry my darling,

I will not write you as the person who always
had all the answers,

that makes you uncomfortable, I know.

But if you'll allow me, I will say this:

When a needle had pierced herself into my skin

I had you to tell me, that when it is over

I will rejoice with safety,

and my day with you will begin.

Chapter 9

I called you yesterday

and you picked up and it was hi how are you?

Oh not much, I just haven't been the same
without you.

I could feel you breathing heavy.

I'm sorry, my darling, I didn't mean to make you
carry

the weight of everything that had happened.

Look, it's complex but it's not.

I've picked up scenarios in my head and
thought,

things in life are always two-way streets.

One has my efforts and the other has my fortune.

But alas I have failed us with my course of
action.

Then I came to say, I'm sorry I love you,

then I woke up.

-       Hello? Are you still there? I can't hear
        you my reception's bad.

Chapter 10

I have written hundreds of poems, letters, and
sayings

that no one may ever read.

I have built a small world within my small world

and what lies between me and this paper is
nothing but my enemy.

The lonely.

You see my darling, the more words I write,

the more you are not there,

the more it is made clear to me,

even when I pour my heart out,

your existence is merely a deceit.

Chapter 11

I see best friends together every day.

But my darling, they do not resemble you,

nor do they resemble me.

They are a fabrication that will never live up to be.

Thinking of you is like magic.

My brain is under the impression that

you are the angel that visits me in the prison that prevents me,

from meeting the people around me.

And finding home in them.

Because magic has a way of showing you

that whatever has been lost,

could be lost again.

-    My dear, I call this piece "Fuck you for the trauma."

Chapter 12

Part 1:

As you may know, my darling,

I have kept myself away from alcohol

It is a sin I rather not.

I have kept myself between a two-line path.

The path that my parents drew for me,

the path that makes me worthy of love,

if I follow it and not stutter outside of it.

I choose the warmth of the path, and not the
treacherous cold of abandonment.

But I promise you this,

if i were to ever lay may hands on beer or wine,

I will drown myself in their passive state;

until my eyes bleed

and my hands grow pale,

Because to avail, they have washed my thoughts
of you

and left me blind.

-       In my cold broken path

Part 2:

I started to paint my darling.

Remember how happy you were when you used
to paint?

My dear readers,

I was always the one that serenaded others.

But I have found so much of her in myself when
I started to draw the art, instead of sing it.

On some days, I have taken care of my brushes.

On others, I have not.

When I'm in pain, I let the minerals eat away the
tips.

When I'm in agony, I clean them and paint until
the canvas drips.

77

So I will sip my wine, and paint.

- This is the part where I tell everyone that I plan
on breaking my paint brushes, but I will not.

- I will write, sing, draw, paint, and dance my
hurt away. Thank-you, dear readers, for making
it this far in my writing.

Chapter 13

If they ever invent time travel

and I get the chance to go back and talk to my younger self,

how will I dare tell myself the horrid truth that is my reality?

How do I look myself in the eye,

and tell myself

that the only person I have ever truly loved and trusted

had left me bare

had left me with more trauma than joy

had left me for other friendships

had left my heart to keep others warm,

And had left me alone?

Before I hit my head on the four walls in my bedroom

trying to answer this goddamn question

Fucking tell me

how can I save myself, from trusting you with myself?

- You had helped me walk, when I took off my wings. But alas, every step I take there is pain.

Chapter 14

I will tell you a secret, my dear readers.

I had sent her a message not long ago,

that reads within the lines of

"I'm still here, I hold no hate for you"

and her response was within the lines of

"thank you for letting me know, I wish you best
of luck."

I had never felt more alone from a message.

The disappointment had struck my heart like
lightning.

But unlike lightning,

the one in my heart will forever stay.

In hopes that if I drown myself in tears

my heart shall feel the electricity it fears.

-	My hurt is naked

Chapter 15

My Dear Readers,

this last page of mine

is not for her, but for you.

If you have felt grief with the pages you read

I am sorry,

my apologies extend to the hereafter

but thank you.

Thank you for taking the time to delve into my
soul with me,

and read out all the words that I never dared to
say.

For me,

it is not the writing that heals this broken side of
me.

It is when I get to share my pain with you, and you share your pain with me.

Because what even is the purpose of art,

when it does not leave people closer to each other, talking to one another, and listening to each other's souls?

Go ahead and share your story, I'm here.

- The End

9 789360 941321